impr 0143448 II game

101 drills
coaching tips and resources

UYK L
(Sa L)

QUANTITY SALES

This book is available at special quantity discounts when purchased in bulk. The book can be used by corporations, organizations or groups for sales promotions, premiums and fund raising. Special imprints, messages or excerpts can be produced to meet your needs. For more information, write to:

Disa Publications
Special Sales Department
350 Ward Avenue, Suite 106
Honolulu, HI 96814.

improve your squash game

101 drills

coaching tips and resources

pippa sales

foreword by Sue Cogswell

DISA PUBLICATIONS

The author and Disa Publications disclaim liability and responsibility to any person or entity with respect to any injury or loss caused or alleged to be caused directly or indirectly by the information herein. If you have any serious medical condition or are taking medications, consult with your doctor before using any of the information contained herein.

IMPROVE YOUR SQUASH GAME
101 Drills, Coaching Tips and Resources

Published by Disa Publications
350 Ward Avenue, Suite 106
Honolulu, HI 96814, USA.
808/923-7179

Cover design: Joan Greenfield, New York
Cover art: Hera Marashian, New York

Library of Congress CIP Data

Sales, Pippa.

Improve your squash game: 101 drills, coaching tips and resources / Pippa Sales
p. cm.
Includes bibliographical references.
Preassigned LCCN: 95-70403
ISBN: 1-884633-03-X.

1. Squash rackets (Game)—Handbook, manuals, etc. I. Title

GV1004.S35 1996   796.34'3
                                QBI95-20410

Printed in the United States of America

10 9 8 7 6 5 4 3 2 1

acknowledgments

Many individuals have generously shared their ideas and time to help make this book an important piece of squash equipment to put in your racquet bag.

Special thanks go to Joan Greenfield for her time and creative talents in designing the cover copy and interior layout. And to Hera Marashian for her cover art.

Bill Barhite, Jonah Barrington M.B.E., Alice Griffin, Quentin Hyder M.D., H.H. Tunku Imran, Susan Jameson, John Nimick, Lisa Opie M.B.E. and Janet Lockrow Richards did a terrific job in reviewing early drafts of the book. Their comments, time and insights are greatly appreciated.

Without Sue Cogswell this book would not be a reality. The years I spent training with Sue on the international circuit allowed me to think of 101 drills and to consider putting them together in a book. A special thanks to Sue for her insights, expertise and support over the years.

To all the players around the world I have been fortunate enough to coach—thanks for allowing me to be your coach and for all I learned from you. Thank you also to all the world-ranked professionals I watched training and playing during my years travelling the international circuit.

The World Squash Federation, United States Squash Racquets Association, Women's International Squash Professionals Association and Professional Squash Association are also thanked for their help.

Finally, this book is dedicated to my mother and grandmother for telling me to "get on with it!" And to my friends around the world whom I have met through squash.

contents

Foreword   15

Introduction: Why Drill?   17

chapter 1   Drilling for Success:
How to Get the Most from the Drills   19

chapter 2   14 Tips to Improve Your Overall Game   23

chapter 3   Service   29
DRILLS 1—2

chapter 4   Return of Service   31
DRILLS 3—4

chapter 5   Forehand and Backhand Drive   35
DRILLS 5—28
- Straight Drive
- Cross Court Drive
- "Put Away"

chapter 6   Boast   43
DRILLS 29—46
- Forehand and Backhand Boast
- Volley Boast

chapter 7   Forehand and Backhand Volley   51
DRILLS 47—69
- Cross Court and Straight Length Volley
- "Put Away"

chapter 8   Forehand and Backhand Lob   59
DRILLS 70—83

chapter 9   Forehand and Backhand Drop Shot   63
                  DRILLS 84—101
                  • Straight Drop Shot
                  • Cross Court Drop Shot

chapter 10   Conditioned Games   71

appendix 1   Stretching Exercises   73

appendix 2   World Squash Federation Affiliated
                  Associations   77

appendix 3   Glossary   89

                  Suggested Reading   93

foreword

Squash is undoubtedly one of the most exacting sports in the world and has continued to grow in popularity since its inception at Harrow School in England in the 1820s.

Like all sports, the game of squash has changed dramatically since the first ball was hit. I am sure that those earlier players would not recognize squash as it is played today.

Technology has bought many advancements to enhance the players' level of play—namely, the racquets, the balls and the introduction of an all glass court which has encouraged more spectators to watch the game. With the game becoming more professional and the rewards ever increasing, players are continually striving to attain higher levels of play.

Gary Player once said that "it's amazing how, the more I practice, the luckier I get." The same is true in any sport: "luck" increases with practice.

Pippa has produced a book which will greatly assist any squash player—from beginner to professional—to achieve that luck. The wide variety of practices makes it interesting and fun. Practicing will never be boring again.

The practices described in this book are a collection of many hours involved in training with me, watching other top players tune their games and in coaching players of all levels. Every player has their favourite practice. Mine is *boast, drive, drive, boast* because it is so versatile and allows your personality to make of it what you will.

Pippa's true love of the game and her involvement as a player, coach and manager has given her a wonderful insight into the game of squash. Through her inherent determination and research expertise, Pippa has put together this collection of practices and resources to make practicing easier and fun.

I hope that you will all enjoy using the book. If you find any other practices you really like, drop Pippa a line.

Congratulations to Pippa on a book expertly written and good luck to you all.

Sue Cogswell
National Director
Squash South Africa;
Five Times British Champion

introduction: why drill?

"Why drill?"

"Having difficulty with a particular shot?"

"Well, practice it!"

You can improve your squash game by practicing the different squash shots in a structured drill situation. When you only play games, your focus is on winning, not on improving a particular shot. Even if you drill only once a week, you will notice an improvement in your game and in your fitness.

Drills provide a controlled situation where a restricted number of shots are practiced at a given time in a set routine. You can have fun practicing and correcting a troublesome shot when it is incorporated into a drill. People who say "but drilling is so boring" have only a limited repertoire of drills which indeed would be boring. Variety is vital to maintain interest. The 101 drills in this book provide that variety.

This book has been designed to be USED! Toss it into your racquet bag. But, remember to take it out and use it! Try some of the drills on your own or with a partner—you will be amazed at how much more fun and beneficial drills are than commonly believed.

Players of different playing levels can often drill effectively together. If your opponent fails to show up, you might find someone of a lesser or greater playing standard with whom you can fill the booked court time. Many of the drills can be also practiced on your own.

Improve Your Squash Game is not a technique book although there are some technique hints to assist you in achieving the shot you are practicing. Rather, the book focuses on improving your shot control, shot selection and shot execution with proper court movement.

To find out more about the game of squash, the rules, court dimensions, type of equipment to buy, in-depth instruction on how to play the game and the personal experiences of the world's top players, read some of the excellent books listed under "Suggested Reading."

Each chapter is divided into a brief description of what you are aiming to achieve in each shot—"Tips"—and how to practice the shot in a drill on your own or with a partner.

I have used all the drills explained either in my personal training or in a coaching capacity. There are more drills and variations on the 101 drills printed here. This book is a guide—a start—to get you enthused about drilling. Expand on the 101 drills or make up your own.

Depending on the part of the world you are from or where you learned your squash, you may be accustomed to the words "practices" or "routines" which mean the same as "drills." I have chosen to use the word "drills" rather than all three words in the text.

The ultimate goal of *Improve Your Squash Game* is to provide you as a player with a necessary tool for improving your game—something positive you can do for yourself—and have fun in the process. Enjoy!

chapter 1

drilling for success:
how to get the most from the drills

- The drills have been designed to improve your stroke
  production, control of the ball and movement to and from the
  ball. A direct result of drilling is that shot selection becomes
  automatic in game situations.

- The drills will help players of all levels. Some drills are easier
  than others. Select drills according to your skill level. Intermedi-
  ate and advanced players will benefit from all drills whereas
  beginners will need to learn basic skills before attempting the
  more intricate drills.

- All drills involve court movement. Some drills are more
  strenuous than others and can, therefore, be used effectively for
  fitness training too. The less strenuous drills are at the beginning
  of each drill section. In drills of unequal function, you need to
  alternate being the feeder so that each player gains the maximum
  from each drill.

- Practice your selected drill for a set time—not until you are tired
  or bored! Vary the drills you practice to maintain your interest
  and to ensure practice of different shot skills. Remember, the
  quality of your practice is more beneficial than endless
  monotonous time spent on the court. If bored, do another drill or
  take a break!

- To make drilling more interesting, score points or set up target
  areas where the ball is to land, or both. Reduce the size of the
  target areas as your skill improves—for example, in drills
  practicing the forehand and backhand length drives, set the

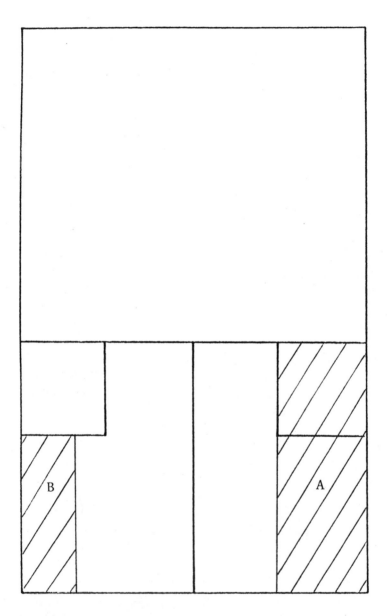

diagram 1   Target Areas
Reduce the size of the target area as your skill
improves.

target area (A) so that the ball must land behind the service line no more than 5.5 feet (1.7m) from the sidewall. As your skill improves, reduce the target area—for example, set the target area (B) so that the ball must land behind the service box and no more than three feet (.9m) from the sidewall. (See diagram 1)

- Some drills cross train shots—for example, in the boast drills other shots are incorporated and therefore practiced as well.

- For rallies in the drills to be continuous, shots should not be outright winners. The exception occurs when the drill incorporates a "put away" or winning shot.

- Unless otherwise expressed, Player A can commence the drill from either the front or the back of the court. Player B starts the drills on the T.

- In the drills that start with a cross court, a service can be substituted to begin the rally thereby practicing the service.

- It is important to discipline yourself to drill on both the forehand and backhand sides. The tendency is to focus on one side at the expense of developing the other.

- The drill sequence of shots is explained once through. "Repeat" after the explanation means that the drill is continuous and played again in the sequence expressed.

- All drills have been explained with a right handed player in mind. If a right handed and left handed player are drilling together, they will be practicing opposite sides at any given time.

- Where the drop shot is used in a drill, it is assumed that a straight drop shot is hit unless otherwise stated.

- Where there are options in a drill and it cannot be stated from which side of the court the next ball is to be hit, the option is expressed as "forehand/backhand."

chapter 2
14 tips to improve your overall game

1 Warm up first, then stretch all muscle groups before playing. Warming up and stretching improves performance and reduces the risk of injury. (See Appendix 1 for stretching exercises.)

2 The foundation of a sound squash game is good length and good width. Hit the ball to stay as close to the sidewall and as deep into the back court as possible. A ball hit close to the sidewall and deep is more difficult to return than one hit into the middle of the court. Play the basics well and you will play a good squash game.

3 "Watch the ball." This means when the ball is behind you too! Watching the ball improves your stroke production and anticipation. Watch the ball right onto your opponent's racquet.

4 "Watch your opponent." If practicing with a partner, focus on watching your opponent so that you develop this skill which then becomes an automatic response in a game situation. Watching your opponent facilitates watching the ball.

5 "Follow through!" This is the most underestimated part of the stroke but an important part of achieving the goal of the stroke. There is time to get your racquet back for the next shot after fully completing your stroke with the correct follow through. A controlled follow through assures a more accurate shot.

6 "Vary the pace of the game." The lob is one way to achieve this. Remember to do it!

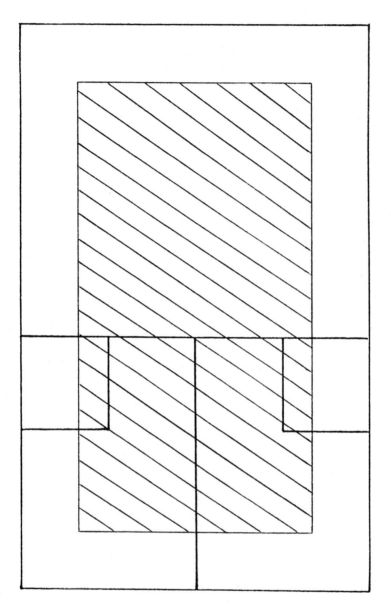

diagram 2   Area of movement on the court.

7 "Use all four corners of the court." It is more tiring to move the full length of the court than it is to move side to side. Use a mixture of shots to move your opponent to all four corners.

8 "Be patient." Choose the right time to go for a winning shot. Hit winners when you have worked your opponent out of position and are balanced to play your winning shot.

9 Play to your strengths and attack your opponent's weaknesses.

10 Eliminate unforced errors from your game.

11 Practice all areas of your game, not just the shots you find easy.

12 "Never give up!" Chase after every ball. Force your opponent to hit another shot. Stay positive. Control the T.

13 "Move back to the T after hitting your shot." Movement to and from the T is critical to hitting a well-executed shot. Restrict your movement to and from the T and the ball to the center of the court. (See diagram 2)

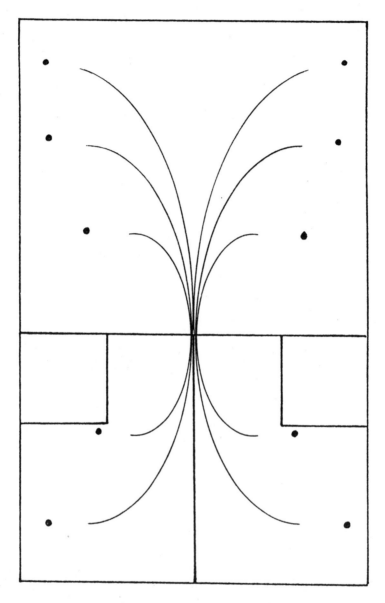

diagram 3   Direction of movement to the ball.

14 "Move to where you want to hit the ball FROM. Do not move directly to the ball." Move down the center of the court, turning to hit your shot when you are almost opposite the ball. By moving down the center of the court, you will find it easier to keep the correct distance from the ball, execute a better shot and conserve energy. (See diagram 3)

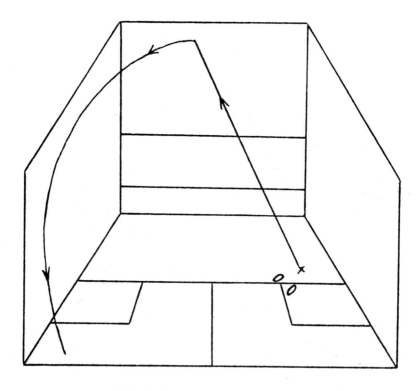

diagram 4   Lob Service from Forehand Court.

chapter 3
service

TIPS

- The service is the only unimpeded shot that you are given. Use it to full advantage and attack any weakness that your opponent may have.

- Take your time before serving. Look to see where your opponent is standing before selecting which type of service you will hit.

- Move to the T as soon as you have struck the ball. This allows you to keep your opponent on the defensive. Don't waste this opportunity!

- The lob service should be played high onto the front wall so that the ball gently touches the sidewall near the back of the court and drops to the floor near the back wall. (See diagram 4)

- The softer and higher the lob service, the harder it is for your opponent to hit. Avoid hitting the service at an acute angle into the sidewall as this will cause the ball to bounce into the court and make it easier for your opponent to return.

- For the lob service, angle your lead foot towards the spot on the front wall where you want the ball to hit. This will help you to hit your target area.

- The hard service is hit slightly above the service line on the front wall, aiming to hit low on the sidewall just behind the service box. Alternatively, to upset the rhythm of your opponent, the hard service can be aimed directly at your opponent or near the center court line.

- Use the same serving position and stance for every service. This will improve your accuracy.

DRILLS ON YOUR OWN

DRILL 1 Having established your target area at the back of the court i.e. the area where you would ideally want the service to land depending on the type of service, hit twenty lob services to this target area from both the forehand and backhand service boxes.

DRILL 2 Having established your target area at the back of the court, hit twenty hard services to the target area (described in drill 1) from both the forehand and backhand service boxes.

chapter 4
return of service

TIPS

- The return of service allows you to regain control of the T and the dominant position. Choose your return of service wisely.

- The standard high percentage return of service is down the sidewall to a good length. (See diagram 5)

- Where possible, take the ball on the volley and before it hits the sidewall as a service that is dropping sharply or one that hits the sidewall is more difficult to return.

- When volleying a service return to a length, the tendency is to take the ball too high. Let the service ball drop a little so that you hit the ball at a comfortable height in the area of maximum control and strength.

- Where to stand to receive service? Roughly one foot (.3m) behind the service box and one foot (.3m) towards the center of the court from the service box. You are now positioned to move in and volley the service or to turn and take the ball off the back wall. Don't get too close to the back wall or sidewall because the walls will impede your swing.

- If a high tight service ball needs to be taken at a height on the sidewall, do not force the return but hit the ball gently back high onto the front wall for an effective lob return.

- Remember to watch your opponent serve. Watch for any clues he or she may give about the type of service he or she is about to play. This will help you to react quickly and play the best return you can.

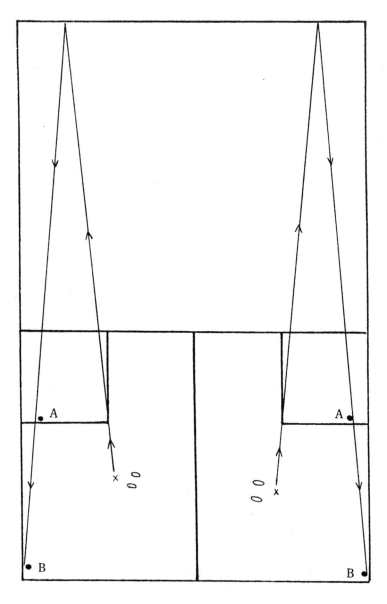

diagram 5   Sidewall Length Return of Service.
A = first bounce of ball
B = second bounce of ball

DRILLS WITH A PARTNER

DRILL 3   Player A hits twenty lob or hard services, or both, from the forehand service box. Player B returns the service down the backhand sidewall to a length. Repeat the drill with Player A serving from the backhand service box.

DRILL 4   Player A hits twenty lob or hard services, or both, alternatively from the forehand and backhand service boxes; Player B hits service returns other than the sidewall length shot e.g. boast, cross court lob, cross court or straight "put aways."

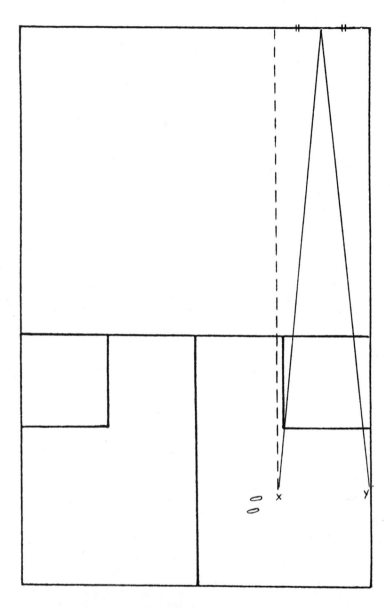

diagram 6   Where on Front Wall to Hit the Ball for a
Forehand Length Drive.
x = Where ball hit from
y = Where ball lands
_____ Path of ball

chapter 5
forehand and backhand drive

STRAIGHT DRIVE; CROSS COURT DRIVE AND "PUT AWAY"

TIPS

• The drive is the foundation of your whole game—the single most important shot in squash.

• For straight drives, the ball should be aimed so that its path is as close to the sidewall as possible.

• The first bounce of the ball should be near the back of the service box so that the second bounce is close to the back wall. The exact spot depends on the height and the speed of the ball and the speed of the court. Force your opponent to hit a weak return—hit your drives deep into the back corners.

• Angle the ball into the back corner. Where on the front wall do you hit the ball to achieve this? On the front wall bisect the line between you at the point you are going to hit the ball from (x) and the sidewall where you want the ball to land (y). (See diagram 6)
  Do not hit the ball too close to the front wall corner as it will hit the sidewall too early and the ball will bounce into the middle of the court. Conversely, the ball, if hit too close to the center line with no angle, will not reach the sidewall.

- To achieve the above aims, there are four factors to focus on—
the correct distance from the ball; shoulder positioning; your
swing; and, the height of the ball on the front wall.

  1   Correct distance between you and the ball is critical. If you
  are too close to the ball you will be unable to swing correctly
  or have your shoulders in the desired position on striking the
  ball. You will lose control of your shot.

  Being too close to the ball is a common mistake—Keep
  AWAY from the ball! The correct distance from the ball is
  greater than you often imagine. It is easier to reach for a ball
  than back away from one that is too close.

  2   Shoulder positioning for straight drives: The ball will travel
  parallel to the sidewall if you keep your shoulders turned to
  the sidewall when striking the ball.

  On the forehand, turn your shoulders parallel to the
  sidewall—so that the line between your shoulders is parallel
  to the path you want the ball to travel.

  As the backhand is played across the body, it is even more
  important than the forehand to keep your shoulders well
  turned to the sidewall and that you step forward with the
  correct foot. It is not possible to swing correctly when
  leading with the wrong foot.

  3   The swing is a complete, free, natural stroke with a full and
  high back swing and an unrestricted follow through along
  the desired path of the ball. It is important not to drop your
  wrist during the swing so that the racquet head stays up
  allowing for the proper execution of the stroke.

  The swing on the forehand and backhand drive can be
  likened to swiftly drawing an imaginary letter U in the air.

  4   Hit the ball high enough on the front wall so that it will reach
  the back of the court. The softer you hit the ball, the higher
  up the front wall you must hit the ball to get it to reach the
  back of the court. Conversely, if your balls are coming off the
  back wall, you are over-hitting; you need to hit the ball lower
  on the front wall.

STRAIGHT DRIVE

DRILLS ON YOUR OWN

DRILL 5 Hit the ball continuously down the forehand sidewall aiming for a predetermined target area in the back of the court. Decrease the size of the target area as your skill improves. Repeat on the backhand side.

DRILL 6 Hit the ball continuously down the forehand sidewall, alternating hitting short and length drives to practice control while moving forward and backwards. Repeat on the backhand side.

DRILL 7 Hit the ball continuously down the forehand sidewall, alternating hitting a hard low drive and then a softer higher drive to allow for recovery. Repeat on the backhand side.

DRILL 8 Hit your drives down the forehand sidewall so that the ball comes off the back wall (over hit). This allows you to drive the ball continuously off the back wall. Repeat on the backhand side.

DRILLS WITH A PARTNER

DRILL 9 Player A feeds a straight forehand short ball from the back of the court; Player B moves from the T to hit a straight length forehand drive. Repeat.

DRILL 10 Player A feeds a cross court short ball from the forehand back court to the backhand side; Player B moves from the T to hit a backhand straight length drive and returns to the T; Player A feeds a cross court short ball from the backhand back court to the forehand side; Player B moves from the T to hit a forehand straight length drive and returns to the T. Repeat.

DRILL 11 Player A hits a forehand boast from behind Player B who moves from the T to hit a backhand straight length drive; Player A hits a backhand boast; Player B moves from the T to hit a forehand straight length drive. Repeat.

DRILL 12 Player A hits either cross court or straight length drives; Player B hits only straight length drives. Repeat.

DRILL 13 Player A hits a forehand cross court length drive; Player B hits a backhand straight length drive; Player A hits a backhand straight length drive; Player B hits a backhand boast; Player A hits a forehand cross court length drive. Repeat.

DRILL 14 Player A hits a forehand boast; Player B hits a backhand drop shot and then hits a backhand straight length drive off own shot; Player A hits a backhand boast; Player B hits a forehand drop shot and then hits a forehand straight length drive off own shot. Repeat. To keep rally going, do not hit drop shot winners.

DRILL 15 Player A hits a forehand cross court length drive; Player B hits a backhand straight length drive; Player A hits a backhand boast; Player B hits a forehand cross court length drive; Player A hits a backhand straight length drive; Player B hits a backhand boast. Repeat.

DRILL 16 Player A hits a forehand straight length drive; Player B hits a forehand boast; Player A hits a backhand drop shot; Player B hits a backhand straight length drive; Player A hits a backhand boast; Player B hits a forehand straight length drive; Player A hits a forehand boast; Player B hits a backhand drop shot; Player A hits a backhand straight length drive; Player B hits a backhand boast. Repeat.

DRILL 17 Player A hits forehand short and length drives; Player B hits forehand straight length drives. Repeat.

DRILL 18 Player A hits either straight or cross court drives to any length or boasts; Player B hits straight length drives. Repeat.

CROSS COURT DRIVE

DRILLS ON YOUR OWN

DRILL 19 Hit one or two straight forehand shots then hit a forehand cross court length drive to a predetermined target area at the back of the court. Repeat on backhand side.

DRILL 20 Hit one or two straight forehand shots then hit a forehand cross court length drive. Move to retrieve your cross court shot. Hit one or two straight backhand shots then hit a backhand cross court length drive. Repeat.

DRILL 21 Hit a forehand straight drive, hit a forehand boast, then hit a backhand cross court length drive. Repeat. To allow the rally to be continuous, retrieve the ball on the second bounce if your shot is too good.

DRILLS WITH A PARTNER

DRILL 22 Player A hits a forehand short straight shot from behind Player B; Player B hits a forehand cross court length drive; Player A hits a backhand short straight shot; Player B hits a backhand cross court length drive. Repeat.

DRILL 23 Player A hits a forehand boast from the back of the court; Player B hits a backhand cross court length drive. Repeat.

DRILL 24 Player A hits a forehand cross court length drive; Player B hits a backhand straight length drive; Player A hits a backhand boast; Player B hits a forehand cross court length drive; Player A hits a backhand straight length drive; Player B hits a backhand boast. Repeat.

SHORT "PUT AWAY"— STRAIGHT OR CROSS COURT

TIPS

- A decisive, "go for it" shot.

- Hit the ball decisively at the top of its bounce.

- To effectively "put away" the ball, aim low on the front wall so that the ball can die in the nick close to the front wall.

- It is easier to "put away" a ball that is closer to the front wall than to the back wall.

- Rallies in the drills will be short if the "dead nick" is achieved.

A DRILL ON YOUR OWN

DRILL 25 Hit a high-bouncing straight forehand shot and then hit a forehand "put away" decisively straight or cross court into the nick. Repeat on backhand side.

DRILLS WITH A PARTNER

DRILL 26 Player A hits a short, high-bouncing straight shot from behind Player B who tries to "put away" the ball straight or cross court into the nick.

DRILL 27 Player A hits a forehand boast; Player B hits a backhand short cross court "put away." If possible, Player A retrieves the "put away" and hits a forehand boast. Repeat.

DRILL 28 Player A hits a forehand cross court drive; Player B hits a backhand boast; Player A hits a forehand short cross court "put away"; Player B hits a backhand cross court if able to retrieve "put away"; Player A hits a forehand boast; Player B hits a backhand short cross court "put away." Repeat.

chapter 6
boast

FOREHAND AND BACKHAND BOAST

TIPS

- The boast is hit into the nearest sidewall. When hitting the boast aim for the forehand front corner of the real or imaginary adjacent court when hitting on the forehand side and the backhand front corner of the adjacent court when hitting on the backhand side. When hit at the correct angle, the boast should land in the nick on the opposite sidewall near the front wall. (See diagram number 7)

- The boast is hit with the same technique as a regular drive but the ball is hit a little later and into the nearest sidewall.

- The attacking or two-wall boast is aimed further down the sidewall so that the ball dies after hitting low on the front wall. (See diagram number 8)

- Do not lift your body or head as you hit the shot. Do not drop your racquet head. Hit straight through the ball.

- Avoid cramping the boast in the back court by keeping OUT of the back corners. You will hit a better shot by reaching for the ball, and not having to back off the ball.

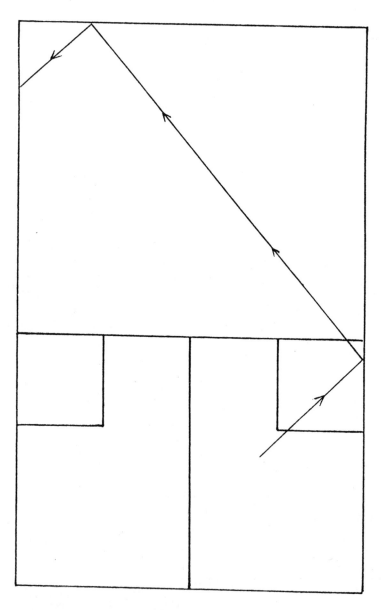

diagram 7   Three-wall Boast.

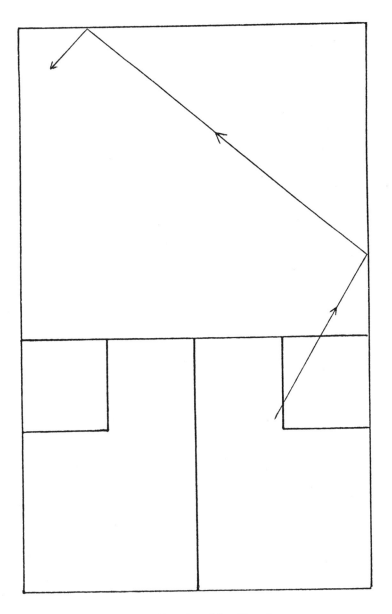

diagram 8   Two-wall or Attacking Boast.

- Boast with an objective—for example, to move your opponent forward—and not for the sake of boasting. A boast is a good shot played at the right time (e.g. when opponent is behind you) but sets you up for trouble when played at the wrong time (e.g. when opponent is in front of you).

DRILLS ON YOUR OWN

DRILL 29   Hit a forehand straight drive down the sidewall then hit a forehand boast off your own shot. Repeat on backhand side.

DRILL 30   Hit two or more forehand straight drives then hit a forehand boast; move to pick up your boast and hit two or more backhand straight drives then hit a backhand boast. Repeat.

DRILL 31   To practice the forehand back corner boast:

a) throw the ball gently onto the back wall (on the forehand side of the court), then hit a forehand boast;

b) throw the ball so it hits the forehand sidewall then the back wall, then hit a forehand boast;

c) throw the ball so it hits the back wall then the forehand sidewall, then hit a forehand boast.

DRILLS WITH A PARTNER

DRILL 32   Player A hits a forehand boast; Player B hits varying length backhand cross court drives. Repeat.

DRILL 33   Player A hits a forehand boast from the back of the court; Player B hits a backhand straight length drive; Player A hits a backhand boast; Player B hits a forehand straight length drive. Repeat.

DRILL 34 Player A hits varying length backhand cross court drives from the front of the court; Player B hits a forehand straight length drive then hits a forehand boast off own shot. Repeat.

DRILL 35 Player A hits a forehand cross court length drive; Player B hits a backhand straight length drive; Player A hits a backhand boast; Player B hits a forehand cross court length drive; Player A hits a backhand straight drive; Player B hits a backhand boast. Repeat.

DRILL 36 Player A hits a forehand cross court length drive; Player B hits a backhand straight length drive; Player A hits a backhand straight length drive; Player B hits a backhand boast. Repeat.

DRILL 37 Player A hits a forehand straight length drive; Player B hits a forehand boast; Player A hits a backhand drop shot; Player B hits a backhand straight length drive; Player A hits a backhand straight length drive; Player B hits a backhand boast; Player A hits a forehand drop shot; Player B hits a forehand straight length drive. Repeat.

DRILL 38 Player A hits a forehand cross court length drive; Player B hits a backhand boast; Player A hits a forehand drop shot; Player B hits a forehand cross court length drive; Player A hits a backhand boast; Player B hits a forehand drop shot. Repeat.

DRILL 39 Player A hits a forehand straight length drive; Player B hits a forehand boast; Player A hits a backhand drop shot; Player B hits a backhand drop shot; Player A hits a backhand straight length drive; Player B hits a backhand boast; Player A hits a forehand drop shot; Player B hits a forehand drop shot. Repeat.

DRILL 40 Player A hits a forehand boast; Player B hits either a backhand straight drop shot or backhand straight length drive; Player A hits a backhand boast; Player B hits either a forehand straight drop shot or a forehand straight length drive. Repeat.

DRILL 41 Player A hits a forehand cross court length drive to start the rally. Player B hits a backhand boast; Player A hits a forehand drop shot; Player B hits a forehand cross court length drive; Player A hits a backhand straight length drive; Player B hits a backhand boast. Repeat.

DRILL 42 Player A hits a forehand cross court length drive; Player B hits a backhand boast; Player A hits a forehand short cross court drive (in front of service line); Player B hits a backhand boast. Repeat.

DRILL 43 Player A hits a forehand cross court length drive; Player B hits a backhand straight length drive; Player A hits a backhand boast or straight length drive; Player B hits a forehand cross court length drive off the backhand boast or a backhand boast off the backhand straight length drive. Repeat.

VOLLEY BOAST

TIPS

- The volley boast is used to attack and put your opponent under pressure.

- The volley boast is hit into the nearest sidewall with the aim of hitting the front wall low and nick on the opposite sidewall near the front wall. You need to hit down on the ball to achieve the nick.

A DRILL ON YOUR OWN

DRILL 44   Hit a high drive down the forehand sidewall; then hit a forehand volley boast.

DRILLS WITH A PARTNER

DRILL 45   Player A hits a high forehand straight drive; Player B hits a forehand volley boast; Player A hits a high backhand straight drive; Player B hits a backhand volley boast. Repeat.

DRILL 46   Player A hits either a high cross court or straight length drive; Player B hits a volley boast. Repeat.

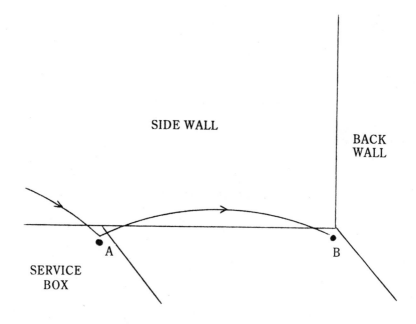

SIDE WALL

BACK
WALL

A

B

SERVICE
BOX

diagram 9   Straight Length Volley.
A = first bounce of ball
B = second bounce of ball

chapter 7
forehand and backhand volley

Cross Court and Straight Length Volley, and Attacking Volley or "Put Away"

CROSS COURT AND STRAIGHT LENGTH VOLLEY

TIPS

- The volley allows you to remain close to the T and gives your opponent less time to prepare and play his or her shot.

- An early back swing is essential for a good volley.

- A straight length volley is most effective the closer it travels to the sidewall.

- The first bounce of the straight length volley should be near the back of the service box so that the second bounce is close to the back wall. The exact spot depends on the height and speed of the ball and the speed of the court. (See Diagram 9)

- Read the last two tips of "The Forehand and Backhand Drive."

- A cross court length volley should die in the opposite back corner.

- Be sure to hit your cross court length volley wide so that your opponent cannot counter volley.

- Hit the ball for the volley as early as you can. The ball can be volleyed at a range of heights varying from knee level to overhead.

- When feeding volleys in the drills, hit a solid shot in preference to a soft lob as it is more difficult to volley a rapidly falling ball.

- Although the feeder wants to extend his or her practice partner in certain drills, do not aim to pass your partner in the volley drills and prevent the opportunity to volley. The more advanced your standard of play is, the wider the ball can be fed.

DRILLS ON YOUR OWN

DRILL 47 Standing near the front of the service box, hit a forehand straight length drive; then, intercept the next length drive and hit a forehand volley to a predetermined target area at the back of the court. Repeat on backhand side.

DRILL 48 To improve your control in volleying down the sidewall, hit consecutive volleys on the forehand side while standing close to the front wall. Then, move a few paces toward the back of the court, hitting several consecutive volleys at each distance until you reach the back wall. Then, move forward again. Remember, this is a flowing rally. Repeat on backhand side.

DRILL 49 To improve your general control of the volley, stand in front of the T and hit alternate forehand and backhand volleys.

DRILL 50 To improve your general control of the volley, stand close to the forehand front corner and hit alternate forehand and backhand volleys, with the ball hitting the forehand sidewall then the front wall, then the front wall then the forehand sidewall. Hit the ball close to the corner for increased control. Repeat on backhand side.

DRILLS WITH A PARTNER

DRILL 51 Player A hits a forehand high straight length drive from the back of the court; Player B moves from the T and hits a forehand straight length volley. Repeat.

DRILL 52 Player A hits a forehand high cross court length drive from the back of the court; Player B moves from the T to hit a backhand straight length volley; Player A hits a backhand high cross court length drive; Player B moves from the T to hit a forehand straight length volley. Repeat.

DRILL 53 Player A hits either a high straight length drive or a high cross court length drive; Player B hits a straight length volley. Repeat.

DRILL 54 Player A hits a forehand high straight length drive from the back of the court; Player B moves from the T to hit a forehand cross court length volley; Player A hits a backhand high straight length drive; Player B hits a backhand cross court length volley. Repeat.

DRILL 55 Player A hits either a high straight length drive or a high cross court length drive from the back of the court; Player B hits a cross court length volley. Repeat.

DRILL 56 Player A and Player B hit straight length drives alternatively down the forehand sidewall. The aim of both players is to try and dominate the T position and stay in front. You achieve this by cutting off the forehand straight length drives with a forehand volley hit to a good length.

DRILL 57 Player A hits a forehand high cross court length drive; Player B hits a backhand straight length volley; Player A hits a backhand straight length volley; Player B hits a backhand boast. Repeat. If you cannot volley the ball, hit a drive to keep the rally continuous and volley when you can.

DRILL 58 Player A hits a forehand high cross court length drive; Player B hits a backhand straight length volley; Player A hits a backhand boast; Player B hits a forehand high cross court length drive; Player A hits a backhand straight length volley; Player B hits a backhand boast. Repeat. If you cannot volley the ball, hit a drive to keep the rally continuous and volley when you can.

ATTACKING VOLLEY—"PUT AWAY"

TIPS

- You want the ball of the "put away" volley to die in the front corners. You can do this more readily by taking the ball in front of your body and aim down so that the ball hits the front wall just above the tin, then the sidewall near the floor or nick.

- A straight "put away" volley is generally the most effective because the ball reaches the front wall more quickly than a cross court short volley and therefore gives your opponent less retrieval time.

- The effectiveness of the cross court "put away" volley is dependent on the position of your opponent and the accuracy of your shot.

- A badly hit straight "put away" volley is more effective than a badly hit cross court "put away" volley which will bounce into the middle of the court.

- The overhead volley "put away" is best played when there is enough time and ball height to prepare for the shot. It is not a shot to be forced—if it is not there, it is not there!

- To achieve the overhead volley "put away," let your racquet head descend rapidly on the ball, hitting the ball hard to land just above the tin and ideally in the nick.

- It is easier to hit a "put away" volley, and attain the correct angle to achieve a nick, when the ball is away from the sidewall.

DRILLS ON YOUR OWN

DRILL 59 Hit up a high forehand ball, then hit a "put away" volley straight into the forehand front corner so that the ball dies. Repeat on backhand side.

DRILL 60 Hit up a high forehand ball; hit a forehand "put away" volley cross court into the backhand front corner. Repeat on backhand side.

DRILL 61 Hit up a number of high forehand length volleys; then select the best shot to hit either a forehand straight or cross court "put away" volley. Repeat on backhand side.

DRILLS WITH A PARTNER

DRILL 62 Player A hits a forehand high straight drive from the back of the court; Player B moves from the T and hits a forehand straight "put away" volley.

DRILL 63 Player A hits a forehand high cross court drive from the back of the court; Player B moves from the T and hits a backhand straight "put away" volley.

DRILL 64 Player A hits a forehand high straight drive; Player B moves from the T and hits a forehand cross court "put away" volley.

DRILL 65 Player A hits a forehand high cross court drive; Player B moves from the T and hits a backhand cross court "put away" volley.

DRILL 66 Player A hits either a high cross court drive or a high straight drive; Player B hits either a straight or cross court "put away" volley.

DRILL 67 Player A and Player B rally down the forehand sidewall with the aim of intercepting the appropriate shot with a "put away" volley either straight or cross court.

DRILL 68 Player A hits up a high forehand ball and then hits a forehand straight or cross court "put away" volley. If the "put away" is not a winner, Player B moves from the T and hits the ball back to Player A's side of the court using a straight or cross court high length drive. Repeat.

DRILL 69 Player A hits up a high forehand ball and then hits a forehand straight or cross court "put away" volley. If the "put away" is not a winner, Player B moves from the T and hits a straight length drive. Repeat.

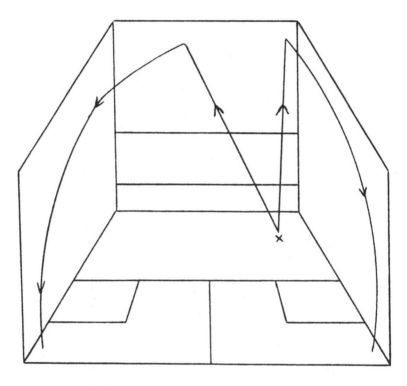

diagram 10 Straight and Cross Court Lob.

chapter 8
forehand and backhand lob

- Use the lob to change the pace of the game and to break your opponent's rhythm. If your opponent likes a fast paced game, slow him or her down by lobbing.

- Use the lob as an effective recovery shot. The lob gives you more time to recover to the T when you are under pressure from your opponent.

- A good lob can change your situation from one of defense to one of attack. The lob helps you to regain control of a rally.

- Persistent and accurate lobbing against a hard hitting opponent effectively tires them.

- A ball dropping down is harder to return than a ball hit hard and straight because you can use the momentum of the hard hit ball. When returning a lob, however, you need to create your own momentum.

- An effective lob is a shot hit high up on the front wall and passes over your opponent's head so that it cannot be intercepted as a volley. (See Diagram 10)

- To obtain the height needed to get the ball high and over your opponent's head, play the ball slightly in front of you with a very open racquet face and hit under the ball with an exaggerated follow through.

- The lob is a shot played DEEP into the back corners. The ball should land behind the service box so that it dies close to the back wall.

- Keep your straight lob tight to the sidewall and high enough to avoid being volleyed by your opponent.

- The cross court lob needs to have both height and width to avoid your opponent cutting it off with a volley.

- When you are in the front court, hit the lob with a short back swing and an open racquet face.

- When you are in the front court, bend your knees and get under the ball to get the lift required to hit an effective lob.

- Remember, play the lob HIGH enough otherwise you will be giving your opponent the opportunity to intercept the ball and gain control of the rally.

DRILLS ON YOUR OWN

DRILL 70 Hit a forehand short shot; then hit a forehand straight lob to a predetermined target area at the back of the court. Repeat on backhand side.

DRILL 71 Hit a forehand short shot; then hit a forehand cross court lob to a predetermined target area at the back of the court. Repeat on backhand side.

DRILL 72 Standing in front of the service line hit a forehand boast; then hit a backhand straight lob or a backhand cross court lob to a predetermined target area at the back of the court. Repeat on backhand side.

DRILL 73 Hit a forehand boast; then hit a backhand cross court lob. Repeat. To have a continuous rally, don't hit winners.

DRILL 74 Hit a forehand boast; then hit a backhand straight lob; hit a backhand straight drive; then hit a backhand boast; hit a forehand straight lob; then hit a forehand straight drive. Repeat. To have a continuous rally, don't hit winners.

DRILLS WITH A PARTNER

DRILL 75 Player A hits a forehand short straight shot from the back of the court; Player B moves from the T and hits a forehand straight lob. Repeat.

DRILL 76 Player A hits either a forehand short cross court shot or a boast from the back of the court; Player B moves from the T and hits a backhand cross court lob. Repeat.

DRILL 77 Player A hits a forehand boast; Player B hits a backhand straight or cross court lob; Player A hits a backhand boast off the straight lob and a forehand boast off the cross court lob. Repeat.

DRILL 78 Player A hits a forehand boast; Player B hits a backhand straight drop shot; Player A hits a backhand straight or cross court lob; Player B hits a backhand boast off the straight lob and a forehand boast off the cross court lob; Player A hits a forehand/backhand straight drop shot; Player B hits a forehand/backhand straight or cross court lob. Repeat.

DRILL 79 Player A hits a forehand straight length drive; Player B hits a forehand boast; Player A hits a backhand straight lob; Player B hits a backhand straight length drive; Player A hits a backhand boast; Player B hits a forehand straight lob. Repeat.

DRILL 80 Player A hits a forehand straight length drive; Player B hits a forehand boast; Player A hits a backhand cross court lob; Player B hits a forehand straight length drive; Player A hits a forehand boast; Player B hits a backhand cross court lob. Repeat.

DRILL 81 Player A hits a forehand straight length drive; Player B hits a forehand boast; Player A hits a backhand drop shot; Player B hits a backhand cross court lob. Repeat.

DRILL 82 Player A hits a forehand straight length drive; Player B hits a forehand boast; Player A hits a backhand straight or cross court lob; Player B hits a forehand/backhand straight length drive; Player A hits a forehand/backhand straight length drive; Player B hits a forehand/backhand boast. Repeat.

DRILL 83 Player A hits boasts and straight length drives: Player B hits straight or cross court lobs off Player A's boasts and straight length drives off Player A's straight length drives. Player A controls the drill by the use of the boast.

chapter 9
forehand and backhand drop shot

STRAIGHT DROP SHOT AND CROSS COURT DROP SHOT

TIPS

- Use the drop shot as an attacking shot to work your opponent or to win the rally outright.

- The drop shot should be aimed to hit the front wall first then the sidewall near the floor or into the nick. (See diagram 11) If the ball hits the sidewall first, the ball will bounce out into the center of the court making the ball easier for your opponent to retrieve.

- The effectiveness of your drop shot increases with deception. Set up as for a drive but hit the drop shot with a shortened back swing.

- An open racquet face on contact with the ball gives you more control when hitting a drop shot and slows the ball down. Putting backspin on the ball also slows the ball down and causes it to drop sharply off the front wall. The follow through is minimal.

- Keep your wrist firm when striking the ball—don't flick the ball.

- A drop shot is most effectively hit off a short ball or a boast. As your skill level increases, you can play a drop shot from anywhere on the court.

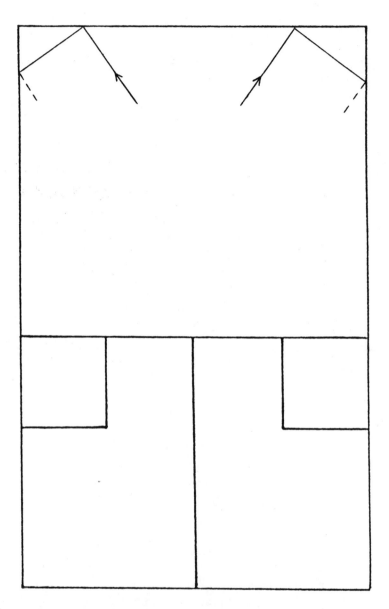

diagram 11   Forehand and Backhand Drop Shot.

- Because the drop shot demands a high level of accuracy, play it when you have worked your opponent out of position and you are well balanced.

- When drop shots are part of multiple shot drills, avoid hitting winners so rallies can be continuous and you can practice both hitting and retrieving drop shots.

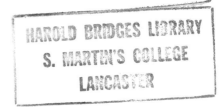

STRAIGHT DROP SHOT

TIPS

- The straight drop shot is effective because the ball has the shortest distance to travel to the front wall and dies quickly giving your opponent little retrieval time.

DRILLS ON YOUR OWN

DRILL 84 Hit a loose forehand straight shot; then hit a forehand straight drop shot. Repeat on backhand side.

DRILL 85 Hit a forehand shot onto the front wall angled so that the ball will hit the sidewall and bounce out into the court; then hit a forehand straight drop shot. Repeat on backhand side.

DRILLS WITH A PARTNER

DRILL 86 Player A hits a forehand straight length drive; Player B hits a forehand boast; Player A hits a backhand straight drop shot; Player B hits a backhand straight length drive; Player A hits a backhand boast; Player B hits a forehand straight drop shot. Repeat.

DRILL 87 Player A hits a forehand straight length drive; Player B hits a forehand boast; Player A hits a backhand straight drop shot; Player B hits a backhand straight drop shot; Player A hits a backhand straight drop shot; Player B hits a backhand straight drop shot; Player A hits a backhand straight length drive; Player B hits a backhand boast. Repeat. Make sure you move off the ball towards the center of the court and back to the T after each drop shot.

DRILL 88 Player A hits a forehand straight length drive; Player B hits a forehand boast; Player A hits a backhand straight drop shot; Player B hits a backhand straight length drive; Player A hits a backhand straight length drive; Player B hits a backhand boast; Player A hits a forehand straight drop shot; Player B hits a forehand straight length drive. Repeat.

DRILL 89 Player A hits a forehand boast; Player B hits a backhand straight drop shot and then hits a backhand straight length drive off own drop shot; Player A hits a backhand boast; Player B hits a forehand straight drop shot and then hits a forehand straight length drive off own drop shot. Repeat.

DRILL 90 Player A hits a forehand straight length drive; Player B hits a forehand boast; Player A hits a backhand straight drop shot; Player B hits a backhand straight drop shot; Player A hits a backhand straight length drive; Player B hits a backhand boast; Player A hits a forehand straight drop shot; Player B hits a forehand straight drop shot. Repeat.

DRILL 91 Player A hits a forehand straight length drive; Player B hits a forehand boast; Player A hits a backhand straight drop shot; Player B hits a backhand straight drop shot; Player A hits a backhand straight length drive; Player B hits a backhand straight length drive; Player A hits a backhand boast; Player B hits a forehand straight drop shot; Player A hits a forehand straight drop shot; Player B hits a forehand straight length drive. Repeat.

DRILL 92 Player A hits a forehand straight length drive; Player B hits a forehand boast; Player A hits a backhand straight drop shot; Player B hits a backhand straight or cross court length drive; Player A hits a forehand/backhand boast; Player B hits a forehand/backhand straight drop shot; Player A hits a forehand/backhand straight or cross court length drive. Repeat.

DRILL 93 Player A hits a forehand straight length drive from the front of the court; Player B hits a forehand straight drop shot from the back of the court. Repeat.

DRILL 94 Player A hits either straight or cross court length drives from the front of the court; Player B hits only straight drop shots from the back of the court. Repeat.

CROSS COURT DROP SHOT

TIPS

- The cross court drop shot needs to be a winner. If not, it opens up the court for your opponent.

- Use the cross court drop shot when your opponent is on the same side of the court as you are and behind you.

DRILLS ON YOUR OWN

DRILL 95　Hit a loose forehand straight shot; then hit a forehand cross court drop shot. Repeat on backhand side.

DRILL 96　Hit a loose forehand shot onto the front wall angled so that the ball will hit the forehand sidewall and bounce out into the court; then hit a forehand cross court drop shot. Repeat on backhand side.

DRILL 97　Hit a few forehand straight length drives; then select the best shot to hit a forehand cross court drop shot from the back of the court. Repeat on backhand side.

DRILLS WITH A PARTNER

DRILL 98　Player A hits a loose forehand short straight shot; Player B moves from the T and hits a forehand cross court drop shot.

DRILL 99　Player A hits backhand cross court drives (varied lengths); Player B hits forehand cross court drop shots. Repeat.

DRILL 100 Player A hits a forehand boast; Player B hits a backhand drop shot; Player A hits a backhand cross court drop shot; Player B hits a forehand straight length drive. Repeat.

DRILL 101 Player A hits a forehand straight length drive; Player B hits a forehand boast; Player A hits a backhand cross court drop shot; Player B hits a forehand straight length drive; Player A hits a forehand boast; Player B hits a backhand cross court drop shot; Repeat.

chapter 10
conditioned games

Now that you have practiced the different shots in squash, practice them in a conditioned game.

What is a conditioned game? In a conditioned game, certain rules and restrictions are attached to the way the game is played. Conditioned games help one or both players to focus on hitting a specific shot repeatedly by either (1) setting a target area or (2) by restricting the type of shots that can be played and by scoring points only by hitting the chosen shots. Or, both restrictions may be imposed. Conditioned games help to reduce unforced errors. The focus is on playing percentage shots.

There are numerous different conditioned games that can be played. Here are six examples of a conditioned game. Make up your own for variety.

EXAMPLES OF CONDITIONED GAMES

1 Player A plays a regular game; Player B can play only a length down-the-wall shot (lob, drive, volley) but may boast out of the back corners if that is the only shot playable. Player B's shots are to land behind the service line. The rally ends and Player A wins the point if the ball lands short of the service line.

   The target area for Player B's shots can be reduced for more experienced players. For example, require the ball to land behind the service box and one foot from the sidewall.

   Player B can, therefore, only win a point or the service by hitting this predetermined target area with a straight length shot.

2 A variation on number 1: Player B has the option of playing cross court length shots only or cross court and straight length shots. Scoring and target areas are the same as for number 1.

3 Both players play regular games but can win a point or service only by hitting a winning drop shot.

A variation on this conditioned game is to have only one player in a given game winning a point or service with a drop shot. Players alternate with the restriction of the winning drop shot.

4 Player A plays a regular game; Player B can hit only straight length drives or boasts and therefore win a point or service off only these shots.

As a variation, Player B can play cross court and straight length drives or boasts.

Restrictions can be placed on Player B's drive shots i.e. predetermined target areas can be set in the back of the court. (See game number 1)

5 Player A or Player B or both play regular games but must lob after a boast or drop shot and automatically lose the point if a lob or drop shot is not attempted. The lob can be either cross court or straight, but deep!

6 Player A plays a regular game. Player B plays a regular game, too, but can only win the point or service by playing a "put-away" volley or volley boast. Players alternate the restricted game.

appendix 1
stretching exercises

Why stretch? Stretching helps to warm up your body for the more demanding task of playing a squash game. Stretching improves your flexibility and helps to prevent injuries. Don't waste precious points by warming up during the first game. Why not take every advantage you can to improve your game? Why give your opponent an unnecessary advantage? Warm up and stretch before you step on court so that you are ready to play your best immediately.

When stretching, don't force your body to go beyond a slight feeling of tension or you may injure yourself. Hold your stretch for about 10-20 seconds. Don't stretch to the point of pain. Be gentle, stretch slowly. Don't bounce up and down as this can cause injury.

There are many stretching exercises and as many ways to do them. Here are thirteen stretching exercises that stretch the main muscle groups used in playing a game of squash:

1   NECK STRETCH

Look over your right shoulder. Hold for 10-15 seconds. Move your head to face directly forward. Pause. Look over your left shoulder. Hold for 10-15 seconds. Repeat five times.

2   WRIST MOBILITY

Rotate your wrists clockwise 10-15 times and then counter-clockwise 10-15 times.

3   CHEST STRETCH

Stand facing a door frame, placing your hands on each side of the doorway at shoulder level. Walk slowly through the door until you feel a slight stretch across your chest muscles. Hold for 10-20 seconds.

4   UPPER BACK STRETCH

Stand facing one side of a door frame, a pole or something fixed that you can grasp at shoulder height. While holding onto the fixed object at shoulder height, lean back and feel the muscles of your upper back stretch apart. Hold for 10-20 seconds.

5   SIDE BENDS

Stand with your feet shoulder-width apart. Lift your right arm overhead with your left hand on your hip. Bend to the left side, feeling the stretch along your right side. Hold for 10-20 seconds. Repeat on the other side of your body.

6   HIP MOBILITY

Place both hands on your hips. Rotate your hips in a clockwise motion for 20 seconds. Repeat rotating the hips in an counter-clockwise motion.

7   FRONT OF THIGH STRETCH

Stand facing a wall a few feet away and brace yourself with your left hand. Lift your right foot up towards your buttocks, holding your ankle with your right hand. GENTLY pull your right foot up closer to your buttocks until you begin to feel tension in your right thigh, and not in your right knee. Hold this position for 10-20 seconds. Lower your right leg and repeat with the left leg.

8 ACHILLES TENDON AND CALF STRETCH

Stand facing a wall with your right foot in front of your left. Your right heel should be about 12-18 inches (35cm-45cm) in front of your left toe. Lean forward placing the palms of your hands flat against the wall at shoulder height. Your right knee should be bent and your left leg almost straight. Move your hips slowly forward until you feel a stretch in the calf of your left leg. Keep both feet and heels flat on the ground. Hold for 10-20 seconds. Then, shift the tension to your left Achilles tendon by bending your left knee slightly while keeping your left heel on the ground. Hold for 10-20 seconds. Repeat with the other leg.

9 HAMSTRING STRETCH (STANDING WITH FEET APART)

Stand with your feet wide apart one in front of the other, toes pointing forward and slightly outward for balance. Bend the left knee while keeping your body weight over your left leg with your chest parallel to the floor. Keep your right leg straight and your hands behind your back. While holding your chest parallel to the floor, slowly straighten the left knee and hold for 10-20 seconds. Be cautious of over-stretching. The stretch should be felt along the back of your left leg. Repeat with the right leg.

10 HAMSTRING STRETCH (STANDING WITH ONE LEG UP)

Stand facing a railing or other elevated surface that is about waist high. Raise your right leg in front of your body and rest your right heel on the elevated surface. Bend forward at the hips leaning your upper body towards your right leg. Hold for 10-20 seconds. You should feel the stretch in the hamstring of the raised right leg and in the lower back. Repeat with the left leg.

11 HAMSTRING STRETCH (SITTING)

Sit on the floor with both legs stretched out in front of your body, knees straight, feet about a yard apart and toes facing straight up. Bending forward at the hips, lean your upper body toward the right leg and grasp your right ankle with both hands. Hold for 10-20 seconds. The stretch should be felt in the right hamstring and lower back. Repeat with your left leg.

12 GROIN STRETCH

Sit on the floor with the soles of your feet together. Hold your ankles to stabilize your position and to pull the heels of your feet toward your groin. Lean forward and with your upper arms or elbows, push against the inside of each knee and push your knees toward the floor. The stretch should be felt in your groin and lower back. Hold for 10-20 seconds.

13 LOWER BACK STRETCH

Lie on your back, raise your right knee to your chest with your knee bent. Hold your right knee with your hands clasped around the knee and pull the right knee toward your chest. Round your lower back as you pull. You should feel the stretch in your lower back. Hold for 10-20 seconds. Repeat with the left leg.

Now, do both legs at the same time – clasp your hand around both knees and pull them towards your chest. You should feel the stretch in your lower back. Hold for 10-20 seconds.

appendix 2
world squash federation (WSF)
member organizations

For more information about squash in your country, including the rules of the game, club locations, tournament schedules for both amateur and professional events contact your National Association.

For those of you who travel and want to play squash in a foreign country, contact the National Association of the country you are visiting. Squash is a terrific way to meet people in different countries who share an interest—squash. Many countries are also eager to host club teams or individuals from other nations.

The names and addresses listed were accurate at the time of writing. If you have difficulty reaching a National Association, contact the World Squash Federation, 6 Havelock Road, Hastings, East Sussex TN34 1BP, Great Britain. Tel: (044) 1424-429245; Fax: (044) 1424-429250.

ANDORRA   Albert Loren, Secretary, Andorra Squash Rackets Association, Centre Esportiu d'Anyos, Principat d'Andorra. Tel: (37) 68-36463; Fax: (37) 68-35035.

ANTIGUA   Susan Dey, Antigua SRA, P.O. Box 901, St. Johns, Antigua.

ARGENTINA   Claudio Guido Fontanazzi, President, Asociacion Argentina de Squash Rackets, Tucamen 255, 4th Floor Ap 'C', CP (1049) Capital Federal, Argentina. Tel: (54) 1-3111575/3134318; Fax: (54) 1-3111575.

AUSTRALIA   Phil Trenorden, Executive Director, Squash Australia, P.O. Box 356, Spring Hill, Queensland 4004, Australia. Tel: (61) 7-38313909; Fax: (61) 7-38316039.

AUSTRIA   Peter Walek, Secretary, Osterreichischer Squash Rackets Verband, Erlachplatz 2-4, A-1100 Wien, Austria. Tel: (43) 1-6041632; Fax: (43) 1-6027404.

BAHAMAS   Paula Rogers, Secretary, Bahamas Squash Rackets Association, P.O. Box F765, Freeport, Bahamas.

BAHRAIN   Mirza Dhait, General Secretary, Bahrain Badminton and Squash Association, P.O. Box 26902, State of Bahrain. Tel: (973) 256321; Fax: (973) 292088.

BANGLADESH   Sohel Kasem, Treasurer, Bangladesh Squash Rackets Association, c/o 1st Floor, 57 Dilkusha C.A. Dhaka 1000, Bangladesh. Tel: (880) 2-259324; Fax: (880) 2-863037.

BARBADOS   Adrian Deane, President, Barbados Squash Rackets Association, P.O. Box 387, Bridgetown, Barbados. Tel: (809) 4359880; Fax: (809) 4359955.

BELGIUM   Denis Permanne, Chairman, Belgium Squash Rackets Federation, Avenue Giele, 43, 1090 Brussels, Belgium. Tel: (32) 2- 426-0896/358-4621; Fax: (32) 2-426-0670.

BERMUDA   Paul Booth, Secretary, Bermuda Squash Racquets Association, P.O. Box HM 176, Hamilton HMAX, Bermuda. Tel: (1-441) 292-6881; Fax: (1-441) 295-5193.

BOTSWANA   Col. N. Clement Mulenga, Botswana SRA c/o Zambia High Commission, P.O. Box 362, Gaborone, Botswana. Tel: (267) 351951; Fax: (267) 353952.

BRAZIL   Eduardo Batista, President, Confederacao Brasileira de Squash, Rua Buenos Aires, 93 Grupo 1208, Centro 20070-020, Rio de Janiero – RJ, Brazil. Tel: (55) 21-2424644; Fax: (55) 21- 2213949.

BRUNEI DARUSSALAM   Mohamed BPSRKDSS Hj Tamin, Honorary Secretary, Brunei Squash Rackets Association, P.O. Box 1279, Gadong Post Office, Mangalait 3112, Gadong, Brunei Darussalam. Tel: (673) 2-23438; Fax: (673) 2-27069.

BULGARIA   Dr. Pluzant Kassablan, General Secretary, Bulgaria Squash Federation, 75 Vassil Levski Boulevard, 1040 Sofia, Bulgaria. Tel: (359) 2865463; Fax: (359) 2879670.

CANADA   Susan Dodge, Executive Director, Squash Canada, 1600 James Naismith Drive, Gloucester, Ontario, Canada K1B 5N4. Tel: (613) 7485672; Fax: (613) 7485861.

CAYMAN ISLANDS   Gillian Lawrence, Secretary, Cayman Islands National Squash Rackets Association, P.O. Box 1504, George Town, Grand Cayman, Cayman Islands, British West Indies. Tel: (809) 949- 7800; Fax: (809) 949-7673.

CHILE   Jose Miguel Prielo, Secretary, Association Chilena de Squash, Los Leones 2008, Providencia, Santiago, Chile. Tel: (56) 2-2258157; Fax: (56) 2-2746283.

COLOMBIA   Sergio Rodriguez, President, Fedesquash, Calle 9. #42-55 of 201, Medellin, Colombia. Tel: (574) 268-0911; Fax: (574) 268-8001.

COOK ISLANDS   Robert Skews, Cook Islands SRA, c/o Island Hopper Vacations Ltd. P.O. Box 240, Raratonga, Cook Islands. Tel: (682) 22026; Fax: (682) 22036.

COSTA RICA   Alvaro Castro, Asociacion Costaricene de Squash, A.A. 3779-1000, San Jose, Costa Rica. Tel: (506) 2280305; Fax: (506) 2897423.

CYPRUS   Ms. Vaso Karasava, Secretary, Cyprus SRA, P.O. Box 7109, Nicosia, Cyprus. Tel: (357) 2-832131; Fax: (357) 2-833892.

CZECH REPUBLIC   Jan Valenta, Chairman, Czech Squash Association, Augustinova 2069, Pr. Schr.46, 148 00 Praha 4, Czech Republic. Tel: (42) 2 2323697; Fax: (42) 2 7932761.

DENMARK   Oluf Jorgenson, Chairman, Dansk Squash Forbund, Idraettens Hus, Brondby Stadion 20, 2605 Brondby, Denmark. Tel: (45) 42-455555; Fax: (45) 42-456245.

ECUADOR   Ivan Palacios, President, Federacion Ecuatoriana de Squash, Av. Juan Tuanca Marengo Km.25, Quito, Ecuador. Tel: (593) 4-8883105; Fax: (593) 4-320051.

EGYPT   Mahmoud Barada, Executive Director, Egyptian Squash Rackets Association, 107 El Tayran Street, Nasr City, Cairo, Egypt. Tel: (20) 2-4100237; Fax: (20) 2-2624273

EL SALVADOR   Ricardo Weisskopf, President, Federacion Salvadorena de Squash, Col. Lomas Verde, Pje Las Rosas #5242, San Salvador, El Salvador. Tel/Fax: (503) 240524.

ENGLAND   Nigel Moore, General Secretary, The Squash Rackets Association, P.O. Box 1106, London W3 0ZD, England. Tel: (44) 181- 746-1616; Fax: (44) 181-7460580.

FIJI   Fay Busuttil, Secretary/Treasurer, Fiji Squash Rackets Association, P.O. Box 14775, Suva, Fiji. Tel: (679) 312844; Fax: (679) 320384.

FINLAND   Poku Salo, Executive Director, Suomen Squashliitto, c/o SVUL, Radiokatu 20, 00240 Helsinki, Finland. Tel: (358) 0- 1582495; Fax: (358) 0-1582411.

FRANCE   Nadla Coste, Admin. Director, Federation Francaise de Squash, 306 Les Bureaux de la Colline, Rue Royale, 92213 St. Cloud, Paris, France. Tel: (33) 1-46-02-70-02; Fax: (33) 1-46-02-70-06.

GERMANY   Rolf Kohnen, Executive Director, Deutscher Squash Verband, Weidenweg 10, 47059 Duisburg, Germany. Tel: (49) 203- 315075; Fax: (49) 203-314813.

GREECE   Dimitris Thilizas, Secretary, Greek Squash Committee, c/o Hellenic Tennis Federation, Athens Tennis Complex, Olympic Stadium, 37 Kifissias Street, 15123 Maroussi, Athens, Greece. Tel: (30) 1-685-2511/2/3; Fax: (30) 1-683-1865.

GUYANA Colin Ming, Secretary, Guyana Squash Racquets Association, c/o The Georgetown Club, 226 Camp Street, Georgetown, Guyana. Tel: (592) 2-61116/60073; Fax: (592) 2-61819.

HONG KONG Heather Deayton, Executive Officer, Hong Kong Squash Rackets Association, c/o Hong Kong Squash Centre, 23 Cotton Tree Drive, Hong Kong. Tel: (852) 28690611; Fax: (852) 28690118.

HUNGARY Dr. Jozsef Kaplar, President, Magyar Fallabda (Squash) Szovetseg, 1146 Budapest, Istanmezeil ut. 1-3 (Kissstadion), Hungary. Tel: (361) 1-805588; Fax: (361) 1-531644.

ICELAND Vladimar Oskersson, Secretary, Iceland Squash Committee, Storhofdl 17, 112 Reykjevik, Iceland. Tel: (354) 1- 682116; Fax: (354) 1-872011.

INDIA Shiv Hazarl, Secretary General, Squash Rackets Federation of India, c/o EG3/11 Garden Estate, P.O. Qutab Enclave, Gurgaon-122001, India. Tel/Fax: (91) 124-351344.

INDONESIA Faried Amir, Secretary, Persatuan Squash Rackets Indonesia, c/o PT Markenin, Hutama, Jin Raya Fatmawati No. 1, Jin Selatan, Jakarta, Indonesia. Tel: (62) 21-7500322.

IRAN Gholam Hossein Farzami, President, Squash Federation I.R. Iran, P.O. Box 15815-1881, Tehran, Iran. Tel: (98) 21-829671; Fax: (98) 21-834333.

IRELAND Maria O'Neill, Development Officer, Irish Squash, House of Sport, Long Mile Road, Dublin 12, Ireland. Tel: (353) 1- 4501564; Fax: (353) 1-4502805.

ISRAEL Dr. Reuven Metrany, Chairman, Israel Squash Rackets Association, Wingate Institute for PE and Sport, Netanya 42902, Israel. Tel: (972) 9-639433-1; Fax: (972) 9-639433.

ITALY Davide Monti, Secretary, Federazione Italiana Giuoco Squash, Via Malteo Tosi 16, 47037 Rimini, Italy. Tel: (39) 541- 790894; Fax: (39) 541-790994.

JAMAICA   Douglas Beekford, Jamaica SRA, c/o Jamaica Trades (Agency) Limited, The Towers, Dominica Drive, 6th Floor, Kingston 5, P.O. Box 316, Jamaica.

JAPAN   Selil Sakamoto, Managing Director, Japan Squash Rackets Association, 2F 2-1-1D Sotokanda, Chi Yo Da Ku, Tokyo, Japan. Tel: (81) 3-52560024; Fax: (81) 3-52560025.

JORDAN   Dr. Hazim Farid, Secretary, Jordan Squash Federation, P.O. Box 3214, Amman, Jordan. Fax: (962) 6-634755.

KENYA   Varun Sharma, Chairman, Kenya Squash Rackets Association, P.O. Box 49751, Nairobi, Kenya. Tel: (254) 2-215334; Fax: (254) 2-332778.

KOREA   Eui Rock Oh, Vice-Chairman, Korea Squash Association, Young Nam Building, 3rd Floor 238-43, Non Hyun Dong, Kang Nam Ku, Seoul 1 35 621, Korea. Tel: (81) 2-545-0012; Fax: (81) 2-516-9413.

KUWAIT   Saleh Al-Enizan Al-Rashidi, Secretary General, Kuwait Squash Federation, P.O. Box 1447, Hawalli, Kuwait. Tel: (965) 2-634618; Fax: (965) 2-655476.

LEBANON   Ahmad Fathallah, General Secretary, Lebanese Squash Federation, P.O. Box 11-3099, Beirut, Republic of Lebanon.

LIECHTENSTEIN   Ralf Wenaweser, Secretary, Liechtenstein SRA, Club Vaduz, Furst-Franz Josef Strasse, FL-9490 Vaduz, Liechtenstein. Tel: (41-75) 232-9686; Fax: (41-75) 235-6501.

LUXEMBOURG   Max Zimmer, Secretary, Federation Luxembourgeoise de Squash Rackets, BP 1255, L-1012 Luxembourg. Tel: (352) 45-6790; Fax: (352) 45-6792.

MACAO   William Kuan, Executive Director, Assgiacao De Squash De Macau, Rua De Joao De Almeida, Macao. Tel/Fax: (853) 338133.

MALAYSIA   Lt. Col. A J Wong, Executive Director, SRAM, P.O. Box 12957, 50794 Kuala Lumpur, Malaysia. Tel: (60) 3-2389960; Fax: (60) 3-389930.

MALTA   Alfred Varsallo, Secretary, Malta Squash Rackets Association, BPO 5, Valetta, Malta. Tel: (356) 242528; Fax: (356) 242224.

MEXICO   Alfredo Martinez Sanchez, President, Federacion Mexicana de Squash, Via A Lopez Mateos # 47, Naucalpan, Edo.Mex., CP 53240, Mexico. Tel: (52) 5-5602921/2608; Fax: (52) 3-360-0556.

MONACO   Patrick Rubino, Secretary, Federation Monegasque de Squash Rackets, 7 Avenue des Castellans, Fontvielle, MC980000, Monaco. Tel: (33) 92-054222; Fax: (33) 92-059437.

NAMIBIA   Neil Thompson, Chairman, Namibian SRA, P.O. Box 153, Windhoek, Namibia 9000. Tel: (264) 61-36308; Fax: (264) 61-63278.

NEPAL   Amar Sinha, President, Nepal Squash Rackets Federation, P.O. Box 257, 15/317 Kaldmara, Kathmandu, Nepal. Tel: (977) 1-211732/215704; Fax: (977) 1-419625.

NETHERLANDS   Rolf de Graaf, Director, Nederlandse Squash Rackets Bond, Postbus 711, 2700 Zoetermeer, Netherlands. Tel: (31) 79- 615400; Fax: (31) 79-615395.

NEW ZEALAND   Grant Scoones, Chief Executive, New Zealand Squash Inc., P.O. Box 21781, Henderson, Auckland, New Zealand. Tel: (64) 98362217; Fax: (64) 98360309.

NIGERIA   Mr. A.B. Dans, Secretary, Nigeria Squash Rackets Association, Nigeria National Stadium, Surulere, P.O. Box 145, Lagos, Nigeria. Tel: (234) 1-5451942; Fax: (234) 1- 15451942/5450104/2691188.

NORWAY Kjartan Tyvand, Executive Director, Norges Squashforbund, Hauger Skole Vei 1, N-1351 Rud, Norway. Tel: (47) 67-154600; Fax: (47) 67-132989.

OMAN Ali s. Al-Bulushi, Secretary, Oman TT and Squash Association, P.O. Box 6778 Ruwi, Sultanate of Oman. Tel: (968) 793089; Fax (968) 793089.

PAKISTAN Flight Lieutenant Muhammad Kurshid, Honorary Secretary, Pakistan Squash Federation, Block No J-11, E-9 Sector, PAF Complex, Islamabad, Pakistan. Tel: (92) 51-85003457/ 51-858761 * 457; Fax: (92) 51-852480.

PANAMA Ramiro Diaz Cabal, President, Confederacion de Squash de Panama, Club Raqueta Panama, A.A. 6-3256, El Dorado, Panama 6. Tel: (507) 60-1986; Fax: (507) 60-0075.

PAPUA NEW GUINEA Lesley Houlston, Secretary, PNG Squash Rackets Federation, P.O. Box 480, Mount Hagen, Papua New Guinea. Tel: (675) 522783/522082; Fax:(675) 521834.

PARAGUAY Dr. Carlos Raul Gutierrez, President, Asociacion Paraguaya de Squash, Edificio Lider V Olivia, 1091 c/ Colon 5 Piso— Of. 52, Asuncion, Paraguay. Tel: (595) 21-492772; Fax: (595) 21- 441936.

PERU Cesar Lazo, Federacion Peruana de Squash, Av. Alfredo Benavides 712. of. 80, Miraflores, Lima, Peru. Tel: (51) 14-442155; Fax: (51) 14-412751.

PHILIPPINES Romeo M. Ribano, President, Squash Rackets Association of the Philippines, c/o 6th Floor Tuscan Building, 114 Herrera Street, Legaspi Village, Mekati, Metro Manila, Philippines. Tel: (632) 818-6995/5448; Fax: (632) 818-5453.

PORTUGAL Steve Walton, National Technical Director, Federacao Potuguesa de Squash, Apartado 9646, 1906 Lisboa codex, Portugal. Tel: (351) 1-8473742; Fax: (351) 1-84778144.

QATAR   Ali Al-Fardan, President, Qatar Tennis and Squash Federation, P.O. Box 4959, Doha, Qatar. Tel: (974) 351629; Fax: (974) 351626.

RUSSIA   Dr. Vasily Borisov, Russian Squash Federation, Luzhnet-skaya nab. 8, 119871 Moscow, Russia. Tel: (70) 95-1630324; Fax (70) 95-9259911.

ST. LUCIA   Maggie Dalton, Secretary, St. Lucia Squash Rackets Association, c/o St. Lucia Yacht Club, P.O. Box 764, Castries, St. Lucia. Tel: (809) 45-28350; Fax: (809) 45-24940.

ST. VINCENT & THE GRENADINES   Cecil Cyrus, St. Vincent & The Grenadines Squash P.O. Box 359, Montrose, St. Vincent.

SAUDI ARABIA   Dr. Mohammed A Seraj, President, Saudi Squash Federation, P.O. Box 57377, Riyadh 11574, Saudi Arabia. Tel: (966) 1-4822731; Fax: (966) 1-4822781.

SCOTLAND   Norman Brydon, General Secretary, Scottish Squash, Caledonia House, South Gyle, Edinburgh EH12 9DQ, Scotland. Tel: (44) 131-3177343; Fax: (44) 131-3177734.

SEYCHELLES   c/o Eric Savy, Squash Liaison Officer, National Sports Council, P.O. Box 580, Mont Fleuri, Mahe, Seychelles.

SINGAPORE   Maj. Hari Nair, Secretary, Singapore Squash Rackets Association, Room 1, Singapore Badminton Hall, 100 Guillemard Road, Singapore 1439. Tel: (65) 3455675; Fax: (65) 3481983.

SLOVAKIA   Ladislav Ochotnicky, President, Slovak Squash Association, Fazulova 2, 81107 Bratislava, Slovakia. Tel: (42) 7- 494444; Fax: (42) 7-495781.

SLOVENIA   Damjan Pintar, President, Slovenian Squash Association, Squash Zveza Slovenjie, Prushnikova 12, 63212 Vojnik, Slovenia. Tel: (38) 63-772620; Fax: (38) 63-772842.

SOUTH AFRICA   Sue Cogswell, National Director, Squash South Africa, P.O. Box 613, Northlands, Transvaal 2116, South Africa. Tel: (27) 11-442-8056; Fax: (27) 11-442-8036.

SPAIN   Paloma Gonzalez, General Secretary, Real Federation Espanola de Squash, c/o Alberto Alcocer 26, 3 1, Madrid 28036, Spain. Tel: (34) 1-4578070/4578795; Fax: (34) 1-4571691.

SRI LANKA   Captain Shanthi Jayamanne, Secretary, Sri Lanka Squash Federation, 2, 18th Lane, Alulhmawatha, Colombo 15, Sri Lanka. Tel: (w) (94) 1-422674; (h) (94) 1-432472.

SWAZILAND   Ray Thomas, Swaziland SRA, P.O. Box 125, Mbabane, Swaziland. Tel: (268) 40553; Fax: (268) 43130.

SWEDEN   Thomas Troedsson, Secretary, Svenska Squashforbundet, P.O. Box 19052, 20073 Malmo, Sweden. Tel: (46) 40- 131969. Fax: (46) 40-138146.

SWITZERLAND   Kuno Ritschard, Executive Director, Schweiz. Squash Rackets Verband, Zugerstrabe 79, Postfach 564, CH-6314 Unterageri, Switzerland. Tel: (41) 42-725457. Fax: (41) 42-725459.

TANZANIA   Col. S.M.A. Kashmiri, Tanzania Squash Rackets Association, c/o Africonsult Ltd., P.O. Box 21242, Dar-es-Salaam, Tanzania. Tel: (255) 51-32299/44811/34097; Fax: (255) 51-31842.

THAILAND   Burapa Atthakor, Vice-President, Thailand Squash Rackets Association, 10 Sukhumvit 31, Bangkok 10110, Thailand. Tel: (66) 2-2604545/4646; Fax: (66) 2-2598448.

TONGA   Peseti Ma'afu, President, Tonga Squash Rackets Association, P.O. Box 1278, Nuku'Alofa, Tonga. Tel: (676) 21041; Fax: (676) 24127.

TRINIDAD & TOBAGO   Joanne Jackson, Secretary, Trinidad & Tobago Squash Rackets Association, c/o #9 Acton Court, Diego Martin, Trinidad, West Indies. Tel/Fax: (809) 6374888.

UGANDA   Derek Banyu, Secretary, Uganda Squash Rackets Association, c/o Bubus International, P.O. Box 2860, Kampala, Uganda. Tel: (256) 41-242487; Fax: (256) 41-250128.

URUGUAY   Enrique Lopez, Federacion Uruguaya de Squash, 25 de Mayo #44, Montevideo, Uruguay. Tel: (598) 295-5302.

USA   Craig Brand, Executive Director, United States Squash Racquets Association, P.O. Box 1216, 23 Cynwyd Road, Bala- Cynwyd, PA 19004, USA. Tel: (1) 610-667-4006; Fax: (1) 610-667- 6539.

VANUATU   Kelera Molloy, Secretary/Treasurer, Vanuatu SRA, P.O. Box 886, Port Vila, Vanuatu. Tel: (678) 23458(w)/ (678) 23902 (h); Fax: (678) 23921.

VENEZUELA   Robert Jones, Caracas Squash Club, Apartado 80057, Prados del Este, Caracas, Venezuela. Tel: (58) 2-241-0066; Fax: (58) 2-241-2551.

WALES   Diane Selley, Secretary, Welsh Squash, 7 Kymin Terrace, Penarth, South Glamorgan CF6 1AP, Wales. Tel/Fax: (44) 1222-704096.

WESTERN SAMOA   Sheree Steklin, Secretary, Western Samoa SRA, P.O. Box 1084, Apia, Western Samoa. Tel: (685) 20331; Fax: (285) 20726.

ZAMBIA   Miss Recreena Banda, General Secretary, Zambia Squash Rackets Association, P.O. Box 70624, Ndola, Zambia. Tel: (243) 2-655529/33; Fax: (243) 2-655059/655534.

ZIMBABWE   Jane Schreiber, Admin. Secretary, Squash Rackets Association of Zimbabwe, P.O. Box CY 162, Causeway, Harare, Zimbabwe. Tel/Fax: (263) 4-790033.

WSF AFFILIATED ORGANIZATIONS

For information about the men's and women's professional tours including tournament scheduling, player information and sponsorship possibilities contact the following organizations:

PSA
(PROFESSIONAL SQUASH ASSOCIATION)

Sheila Cooksley, Tour Director, Professional Squash Association, 82 Cathedral Road, Cardiff CF1 9LN, Wales. Tel: (44) 1222-388446; Fax: (44) 1222-228185.

John Nimick, Executive Director, Professional Squash Association, 56 Spooner Road, Chestnut Hill, MA 02167, USA. Tel: (1) 617-7316874; Fax: (1) 617-2771457.

WISPA
(WOMEN'S INTERNATIONAL SQUASH PLAYERS ASSOCIATION)

Andrew Shelley, Executive Director, or Heather Mills, Administrator, Women's International Squash Players Association, 27 Westminster Palace Gardens, Artillery Row, Victoria, London SW1P 1RR, England. Tel: (44) 171-976-6660; Fax: (44) 171-976-8778.

appendix 3
glossary

Angle shot   A shot played where the ball first hits the sidewall and then the front wall, or vice versa.

Appeal   A request to the referee for a let, a penalty or to query the decision of the marker.

Back spin or slice   Spin added to the ball by slicing the racquet beneath the ball.

Basic game   This implies the basic tactical ingredients of the squash game.

Boast   An angle shot played so that the ball hits the sidewall before hitting the front wall.

Closed racquet face   When the forward face of the racquet is turned slightly from the vertical position towards the floor, the racquet face is said to be closed. This causes the ball to be hit on a more downward path.

Closed stance   This is the classic approach used to drive a squash ball—the player approaches the ball side-on, with the front foot forward and the shoulders parallel to the sidewall.

Correct foot   A right handed player should step forward on the left foot for a forehand shot and on the right foot for a backhand shot. A left handed player should step forward on the right foot for a forehand shot and on the left foot for a backhand shot.

Cross court shot A shot hit at such an angle to the front wall that it returns to the opposite side of the court.

Cut line The horizontal red wall marking on the front wall, 6 feet or 1.829 meters above the floor, and extending the full width of the court. The service must be hit above this line.

Deep A ball hit far into the back of the court.

Dies The ball dies when it lacks sufficient momentum to bounce and cannot be returned.

Down The call made when a shot fails to clear the tin.

Drop shot A shot played delicately onto the front wall just above the tin and angled toward a sidewall.

Game Ball The state of the score when the server requires one more point to win the game in progress.

Half-court line A line set out upon the floor parallel to the sidewalls, dividing the back of the court into two equal parts, meeting the short line at its midpoint to form the "T".

Hand The period from the time a player becomes server until he becomes receiver.

Hand-in The player who serves.

Hand-out The player receiving service; also the term used to indicate that hand-in has become hand-out.

Kill shot An aggressive shot played hard and low to win the rally.

Length Any shot that is played deep into the back of the court.

Let When a rally has to be played again due to one or both players being impeded.

Lob A delicate shot that sends the ball high and wide over an opponent's head to land at the back of the court.

Match ball   The state of the score when the server requires one point to win the match.

Nick   The area of the court where the floor and the side wall join.

Not up   The expression used to indicate that the ball has not been hit in accordance with the rules.

Open racquet face   When the forward face of the racquet is turned slightly from the vertical position towards the ceiling the racquet face is said to be open. This causes the ball to be hit on a more upward path.

Open stance   When a shot is played with most of the chest facing the front wall.

Out   The ball is out when it touches the out-line or hits the wall above the out-line or passes over any cross bars or other part of the roof of the court.

Out line   The red wall marking that forms the upper limit of the court on all four walls. Any ball hitting this line or the wall above it, is out.

Percentage game   A player plays only those shots of which the player is unlikely to make an error.

"Put Away"   An aggressive shot played hard and low to win the rally.

Rally   The time that the ball is in constant play, ending when one player hits the ball out of court or fails to make a return or makes an illegal move.

Service   The method by which the ball is put into play by the server to commence a rally.

Service box or box   A square area in each quarter court bounded by part of the short line, part of the sidewall and by two other lines, and from within which the server serves.

Short line   A line set out upon the floor parallel to and 18 feet or 5.486 meters from the front wall and extending the full width of the court.

"T"   The junction of the half court line and the short line. Strategically, it is the most important area on the court.

Tin   The lowest horizontal marking on the front wall—19 inches or .484 meters from the floor. The ball must be hit above this line for the shot to be good.

Working an opponent   The strategy of playing a variety of shots causing your opponent to run around the court as much as possible.

Volley   A shot that is hit before the ball has bounced off the floor.

suggested reading

Another "tip" for improving your squash game is to read what squash experts around the world have written. The suggested reading list will expose you to books ranging from the history of squash to the technique of all squash shots to game strategy as used by World Champions.

If you have difficulty finding a book, contact The Squash Connection—(813) 489-1677—they offer many of the listed books for sale. Also, the monthly newspaper Squash News—186 Arcadia Road, Hope Valley, RI 02832, (401) 539-2381—contains the latest information on what's happening in the squash world.

Barnaby, Jack, *Winning Squash Racquets*, Allyn & Bacon, Boston, 1979.

Barrington, Jonah, *Barrington On Squash*, Stanley Paul & Co. Ltd., London, 1974.

Barrington, Jonah, *Squash in Action*, Stanley Paul & Co. Ltd., London, 1986.

Bellamy, Rex, *The Story of Squash*, Cassell Ltd., London, 1978.

Bellamy, Rex, *Squash a History*, Heinemann Kingswood, London, 1987.

Brownlee, Colin, *Introduction to Squash Training: The Brownlee Way*, Squash World International Limited, Rotorua, New Zealand, 1979, 1984.

Brownlee, Colin, *Squash: The Brownlee Way*, Squash World International Limited, Rotorua, New Zealand, 1984.

Chapman, Claire, *Teaching Squash*, G. Bell & Sons Ltd., London, 1976.

Colburn, Alan, *Squash: The Ambitious Player's Guide*, Faber & Faber Ltd., London, 1981.

Constable, Betty; Peck, Norman and White,Dan, *Squash Basics for Men and Women*, Hawthorn Books, New York, 1979.

Dardir and Gilmour, Garth, *Dardir on Squash*, Gilmour Associates, Auckland, New Zealand, 1971:

Francis, Austin, *Smart Squash: How to Win at Soft Ball*, Lions and Burford, New York, 1995.

Goodall, Penny, *A Guide to Group Coaching*, WSRA, London, 1979.

Hawkey, Dick, *Starting Squash*, Ward Locke Ltd., London, 1975.

Hunt, Geoff, *Geoff Hunt on Squash*, Cassell Ltd., London, 1974.

Khan, Hashim with Richard Randall, *Squash Racquets: The Khan Game*, Wayne State University Press, Detroit, 1967.

Khan, Jehangir with Rahmat Khan and Richard Eaton, *Winning Squash*, Stanley Paul and Company, Ltd., London, 1985.

Khan, Jehangir, *Learn Squash and Racquetball in a Weekend*, Alfred A. Knopf, New York and Dorling Kindersley, London, 1993.

Lindsey, Crawford W. Jr., *The Book of Squash: A Total Approach to the Game*, Taylor Publishing, Dallas, 1987.

McKay, Heather, *Complete Book of Squash*, Macmillan Co. Of Canada Ltd., Toronto, 1977.

McKenzie, Ian, *The Squash Workshop: A Complete Game Guide*, Crowood Press Ltd., Ramsbury Marlborough, England, 1993.

Pearson, David, *Ahead of the Game: Squash*, Ward Lock, London, 1990.

Sommers, Eric, *Squash: Technique, Tactics, Training*, Crowood Press Ltd., Ramsbury Marlborough, England, 1991.

Squash Rackets Association, *Squash Guide*, Filofax Ltd., Ilford, England, 1990.

Taylor, John, *Squash: Top Coach*, Pelham Books Ltd., London,1985

order form

Here's how to buy additional copies of *Improve Your Squash Game: 101 Drills, Coaching Tips and Resources*:

- Purchase a copy at your local bookstore

- Call 1-800-35-BOOKS (1-800-352-6657) 24 hours a day, 7 days a week. Visa and Mastercard accepted.

- Mail check or money order to:
  Disa Publications
  350 Ward Avenue, Suite 106, Honolulu, HI 96814
  (808) 923-7179
  or
  The Squash Connection
  Rainmaker Building, 2290 Bruner Lane, Ft. Myers, FL 33912
  (813) 489-1677

Please send _____ copies of *Improve Your Squash Game: 101 Drills, Coaching Tips and Resources* at $13.95 each

NAME _____

ADDRESS _____

CITY/STATE/ZIP _____

DAYTIME PHONE _____

Shipping (within the United States)
Disa Publication rates:
  Book rate: $2.00 for the first book and $1.00 for each additional book.
    (Surface shipping may take 3-4 weeks)
  Air Mail: $3.00 for the first book and $1.50 for each additional book.
Contact The Squash Connection for their shipping rates.

Quantity discounts are available. For details, please contact
Disa Publications, 350 Ward Avenue, Suite 106, Honolulu, HI 96814.

Call toll free and order now.